Better Homes and Gardens.

Best-Loved Desserts

Easy Everyday Recipe Library

BETTER HOMES AND GARDENS® BOOKS

Des Moines, Iowa

EASY EVERYDAY RECIPE LIBRARY
Better Homes and Gardens® Books, An imprint of Meredith® Books
Published for Creative World Enterprises LP, West Chester, Pennsylvania
www.creativeworldcooking.com

Best-Loved Desserts
Project Editors: Spectrum Communication Services, Inc.
Project Designers: Seif Visual Communications
Copy Chief: Catherine Hamrick
Copy and Production Editor: Terri Fredrickson
Contributing Proofreaders: Kathy Eastman, Susan J. Kling
Electronic Production Coordinator: Paula Forest
Editorial and Design Assistants: Judy Bailey, Mary Lee Gavin, Karen Schirm
Test Kitchen Director: Lynn Blanchard
Production Director: Douglas M. Johnston
Production Managers: Pam Kvitne, Marjorie J. Schenkelberg

Meredith® Books
Editor in Chief: James D. Blume
Design Director: Matt Strelecki
Managing Editor: Gregory H. Kayko

Director, Sales & Marketing, Retail: Michael A. Peterson
Director, Sales & Marketing, Special Markets: Rita McMullen
Director, Sales & Marketing, Home & Garden Center Channel: Ray Wolf
Director, Operations: George A. Susral

Vice President, General Manager: Jamie L. Martin

Better Homes and Gardens® Magazine
Editor in Chief: Jean LemMon
Executive Food Editor: Nancy Byal

Meredith Publishing Group
President, Publishing Group: Christopher M. Little
Vice President, Consumer Marketing & Development: Hal Oringer

Meredith Corporation
Chairman and Chief Executive Officer: William T. Kerr

Chairman of the Executive Committee: E. T. Meredith III

Creative World Enterprises LP
Publisher: Richard J. Petrone
Design Consultants to Creative World Enterprises: Coastline Studios, Orlando, Florida

All of us at Better Homes and Gardens® Books are dedicated to providing you with the information and ideas you need to create delicious foods. We welcome your comments and suggestions. Write to us at: Better Homes and Gardens Books, Cookbook Editorial Department, 1716 Locust St., Des Moines, Iowa 50309-3023.

Our seal assures you that every recipe in *Best-Loved Desserts* has been tested in the Better Homes and Gardens® Test Kitchen. This means that each recipe is practical and reliable, and meets our high standards of taste appeal. We guarantee your satisfaction with this book for as long as you own it.

Cover photo: Cheesecake Supreme
(see recipe, page 22)

Is a rich, homemade dessert your idea of paradise?
Then you've come to the right place! Sweet dreams are made of
the recipes found within the covers of *Best-Loved Desserts.*

Try dazzling delights such as cheesecakes or meringues that
fit the most elegant occasion. Or, choose from such
comforting favorites as fruit cobblers, chewy cookies,
and fresh-from-the-oven pies.

So, go ahead. Let visions of sugar plums dance through
your head as you page through this dessert-lover's dream book.

CONTENTS

Peach Cobbler with Cinnamon-Swirl Biscuits

Many cobbler recipes have a drop biscuit topping, but this one has tender biscuit slices filled with a nut-and-spice mixture.

1 cup all-purpose flour
1 tablespoon brown sugar
1½ teaspoons baking powder
¼ teaspoon salt
⅛ teaspoon baking soda
¼ cup butter
⅓ cup milk
½ cup finely chopped walnuts
3 tablespoons brown sugar
¼ teaspoon ground cinnamon
1 tablespoon butter, melted
⅔ cup packed brown sugar
4 teaspoons cornstarch
½ teaspoon finely shredded
   lemon peel
6 cups sliced peeled peaches or
   6 cups frozen unsweetened
   peach slices
⅔ cup water

For biscuits, in a medium mixing bowl stir together flour, 1 tablespoon brown sugar, baking powder, salt, and baking soda. With a pastry blender, cut in ¼ cup butter till the mixture resembles coarse crumbs. Make a well in the center. Add milk all at once. Using a fork, stir just till dough forms a ball.

On a lightly floured surface, knead dough gently for 10 to 12 strokes. Roll or pat dough into a 12x6-inch rectangle. Combine walnuts, 3 tablespoons brown sugar, and cinnamon. Brush dough with melted butter and sprinkle with nut mixture. Starting from a short side, roll up jelly-roll style. Seal edge. Cut into six 1-inch slices. Set aside.

For filling, in a large saucepan stir together ⅔ cup brown sugar, cornstarch, and lemon peel. Add peaches and water. Cook and stir till thickened and bubbly. Pour hot filling into an ungreased 2-quart rectangular baking dish. Arrange biscuit slices, cut sides down, on hot filling. Bake in a 375° oven about 25 minutes or till biscuits are golden. Makes 6 servings.

Nutrition information per serving: 436 calories, 5 g protein, 71 g carbohydrate, 17 g fat (3 g saturated), 13 mg cholesterol, 315 mg sodium.

Apple-Walnut Cobbler

The tastes of autumn come alive in this homespun dessert featuring slices of tart apples topped with walnuts and cinnamon and served with whipped cream or ice cream.

5   cups thinly sliced peeled
      cooking apples
¾   cup chopped walnuts
¼   cup sugar
½   teaspoon ground cinnamon
1   cup all-purpose flour
½   cup sugar
1   teaspoon baking powder
1   beaten egg
½   cup evaporated milk
⅓   cup butter or margarine, melted
      Whipped cream or vanilla ice cream
        (optional)
      Ground cinnamon (optional)

Lightly grease a 2-quart square baking dish. Spread apples in prepared dish. Sprinkle with ½ cup of the walnuts. In a small bowl stir together ¼ cup sugar and ½ teaspoon cinnamon; sprinkle over apples.

In a medium mixing bowl stir together flour, ½ cup sugar, and baking powder. In a small mixing bowl combine the egg, evaporated milk, and melted butter or margarine. Stir into flour mixture till smooth. Pour evenly over apples; sprinkle with remaining walnuts.

Bake in a 325° oven for 50 to 55 minutes or till a wooden toothpick inserted in center comes out clean. To serve, cut into squares. Serve warm. If desired, top with whipped cream or ice cream and sprinkle with additional cinnamon. Makes 9 servings.

Nutrition information per serving: 304 calories, 5 g protein, 41 g carbohydrate, 15 g fat (6 g saturated), 46 mg cholesterol, 143 mg sodium.

Country Pear and Cherry Crisp

The topping stays extra-crunchy, and the best part is that it's a simple combination of granola and butter.

1 16-ounce package frozen unsweetened pitted tart red cherries, thawed, or one 16-ounce can pitted tart red cherries (water pack)

⅓ to ½ cup sugar

2 tablespoons all-purpose flour

1 teaspoon finely shredded orange peel

½ teaspoon ground cinnamon

3 to 4 medium pears, peeled, cored, and thinly sliced (3 cups)

1½ cups granola

2 tablespoons butter, melted
   Vanilla ice cream (optional)

If using canned cherries, drain cherries, reserving ½ cup juice. In a large mixing bowl combine frozen or canned cherries and reserved juice. Add sugar and toss to coat. Let stand for 5 minutes.

Combine flour, orange peel, and cinnamon. Sprinkle over cherries; toss to mix. Add pears; toss to mix. Transfer to an ungreased 2-quart square baking dish. Combine granola and butter; sprinkle over filling. Bake in a 375° oven about 30 minutes or till pears are tender. If necessary, cover with foil the last 5 to 10 minutes to prevent overbrowning. Serve warm. If desired, serve with ice cream. Makes 6 servings.

Nutrition information per serving: 318 calories, 4 g protein, 58 g carbohydrate, 10 g fat (4 g saturated), 5 mg cholesterol, 94 mg sodium.

Gingered Shortcake with Spiced Fruit

Shortcake isn't just for summer berries anymore! Enjoy this warming dessert with fall fruits such as apples, persimmons, or pears. The shortcake can be made ahead and refrigerated, then warmed—wrapped in foil— in a 350° oven about 25 minutes.

Gingered Shortcake
1 cup whipping cream
2 tablespoons granulated sugar
½ teaspoon vanilla
3 tablespoons butter
3 medium cooking apples, Fuyu
   persimmons, and/or pears, cored
   (if necessary) and thinly sliced
3 tablespoons brown sugar
¼ teaspoon ground nutmeg
1 cup blueberries

Prepare Gingered Shortcake. In a chilled bowl combine cream, granulated sugar, and vanilla. Beat with chilled beaters of an electric mixer till soft peaks form. Cover and chill.

In a large skillet melt butter over medium heat. Add apples, persimmons, and/or pears. Cook for 2 to 5 minutes or till almost tender. Stir in brown sugar and nutmeg. Cook for 1 to 3 minutes more or till tender. Stir in blueberries.

Place bottom cake layer on serving plate. Spoon about two-thirds of the fruit mixture and half of the whipped cream over cake. Top with second cake layer and remaining fruit mixture. Pass remaining whipped cream. Makes 8 servings.

Gingered Shortcake: Combine 2 cups *all-purpose flour*, ¼ cup *granulated sugar*, and 2 teaspoons *baking powder*. Cut in ½ cup *butter* till mixture resembles coarse crumbs. Combine 1 beaten *egg*, ⅔ cup *milk*, and 1 tablespoon grated *gingerroot;* add to flour mixture. Stir just to moisten. Spread in a greased 8x1½-inch round baking pan. Bake in a 450° oven for 18 to 20 minutes or till a wooden toothpick inserted near the center comes out clean. Cool in pan for 10 minutes. Remove from pan; cool on a wire rack for 30 minutes. Split into 2 layers.

Nutrition information per serving: 457 calories, 5 g protein, 47 g carbohydrate, 28 g fat (17 g saturated), 111 mg cholesterol, 280 mg sodium.

Red Wine-Marinated Peaches

Embellish this golden fruit with red wine, cinnamon, and cloves.

6 ripe medium peaches, peeled, pitted, and sliced, or pears, cored and sliced

1½ cups fruity red wine (such as Beaujolais) or dry white wine

¾ cup sugar

½ teaspoon ground cinnamon

⅛ teaspoon ground cloves

Place peaches or pears in a large bowl. For marinade, in a medium saucepan combine the wine, sugar, cinnamon, and cloves. Cook and stir over medium heat till sugar is dissolved.

Pour the marinade over peaches; toss gently to coat. Marinate at room temperature for 30 to 60 minutes, stirring occasionally. To serve, spoon the peaches and marinade into dessert dishes. Makes 6 servings.

Nutrition information per serving: 262 calories, 1 g protein, 51 g carbohydrate, 0 g fat (0 g saturated), 0 mg cholesterol, 6 mg sodium.

Chilled Fruit Soup

Swirled with a little sweetened whipped cream, fruit soup makes a sensational ending to a nice meal.

4 cups seasonal fruit (such as blueberries, raspberries, and/or cut-up cantaloupe, honeydew melon, or strawberries)

1 8-ounce carton plain low-fat yogurt

½ cup sugar

3 tablespoons lemon juice

¼ cup whipping cream

1 teaspoon sugar

In a blender container or food processor bowl combine half of the fruit, half of the yogurt, ¼ cup of the sugar, and 2 tablespoons of the lemon juice. Cover and blend or process till smooth. Strain through a fine sieve into a large storage container. Repeat with the remaining fruit, remaining yogurt, ¼ cup of the sugar, and remaining lemon juice. Add to the first batch. Cover and chill for 4 to 24 hours.

Before serving, in a chilled small bowl combine cream and 1 teaspoon sugar. Beat with chilled beaters of an electric mixer till soft peaks form. To serve, stir soup, then divide among dessert bowls. Swirl whipped cream into each serving. Makes 4 to 6 servings.

Nutrition information per serving: 251 calories, 4 g protein, 46 g carbohydrate, 7 g fat (4 g saturated), 24 mg cholesterol, 52 mg sodium.

Pineapple-Orange Crepes

If you like, make the crepes up to 2 days before serving them. Stack them with waxed paper between the layers and store in an airtight container in the refrigerator.

½ cup all-purpose flour
⅓ cup milk
½ teaspoon finely shredded orange peel
⅓ cup orange juice
1 egg
2 teaspoons cooking oil
½ of a fresh pineapple, peeled, cored, and sliced
2 tablespoons butter or margarine
¼ cup packed brown sugar
1 tablespoon cornstarch
½ cup orange juice
2 medium oranges, peeled and sectioned
1 tablespoon rum (optional)
¼ cup chopped pecans or slivered almonds, toasted
¼ cup coconut, toasted
Fresh strawberries (optional)

For crepes, in a small mixing bowl combine flour, milk, orange peel, ⅓ cup orange juice, egg, and oil. Beat with a rotary beater till well mixed. Heat a lightly greased 6-inch skillet over medium heat. Spoon 2 tablespoons of the batter into the skillet; lift and tilt the skillet to spread batter. Return to heat; brown on one side only. Invert pan over paper towels; remove crepe. Repeat with the remaining batter, greasing skillet occasionally.

Fold each crepe in half, browned side out. Fold in half again, forming a triangle. Place in a single layer on a baking sheet. Keep crepes warm in a 300° oven while making the sauce.

For sauce, cut the pineapple slices into fourths; set aside. In a medium saucepan melt butter or margarine. Stir in brown sugar and cornstarch. Add ½ cup orange juice. Cook and stir till thickened and bubbly. Cook and stir for 1 minute more. Add pineapple, orange sections, and, if desired, rum. Cook over low heat, stirring gently, till heated through.

Arrange folded crepes on dessert plates. Spoon sauce over crepes. Sprinkle with nuts and coconut. If desired garnish with fresh strawberries. Makes 4 servings.

Nutrition information per serving: 345 calories, 6 g protein, 45 g carbohydrate, 17 g fat (5 g saturated), 70 mg cholesterol, 102 mg sodium.

Gingered Melon

Enjoy this cool, refreshing melon cup on the hottest days of summer.

¾ cup water
½ cup sugar
2 teaspoons finely shredded lemon
    peel (set aside)
4 teaspoons lemon juice
1½ to 2 teaspoons grated gingerroot
4 cups watermelon, cantaloupe,
    and/or honeydew melon balls
⅓ cup flaked coconut

For syrup, in a small saucepan combine water, sugar, lemon juice, and gingerroot. Bring to boiling; reduce heat. Simmer, uncovered, for 3 minutes. Remove from heat; stir in lemon peel. Cool to room temperature. If desired, strain syrup. Pour over melon. Stir gently to coat. Cover and chill for 2 to 24 hours.

To serve, spoon melon and syrup into dessert dishes. Sprinkle with coconut. Makes 6 servings.

Nutrition information per serving: 122 calories, 1 g protein, 28 g carbohydrate, 2 g fat (1 g saturated), 0 mg cholesterol, 10 mg sodium.

Honey-Fruit Pizza

Pretty as a picture, this fresh-tasting masterpiece features a cookie crust, summer fruits, and a honey glaze.

¾ cup butter or margarine
⅓ cup sifted powdered sugar
2 cups all-purpose flour
2 tablespoons honey
1 tablespoon cornstarch
⅓ cup apple or orange juice
2 tablespoons currant or apple jelly
1 cup sliced strawberries
1 medium nectarine, pitted and
    sliced, or 1 medium peach,
    peeled, pitted, and sliced
½ cup blueberries or raspberries
½ cup seedless green or red grapes,
    halved

For crust, beat butter or margarine with an electric mixer on medium speed for 30 seconds. Beat in the powdered sugar. Gradually add flour, beating till well mixed. Pat into a greased 11- or 12-inch pizza pan. Bake in a 375° oven for 15 to 18 minutes or till golden. Cool in pan on a wire rack.

For glaze, stir together honey and cornstarch. Stir in juice and jelly. Cook and stir till thickened and bubbly. Cook and stir for 2 minutes more. Remove from heat. Cool for 5 minutes (do not stir). Spread half of the glaze onto crust. Top with fruit and the remaining glaze. Chill at least 30 minutes before serving. Makes 12 servings.

Nutrition information per serving: 223 calories, 2 g protein, 28 g carbohydrate, 12 g fat (7 g saturated), 31 mg cholesterol, 118 mg sodium.

Gingered Melon

Cream Cheese-Poppy Seed Pound Cake

Cream cheese and butter team up to ensure a moist texture and rich flavor in this melt-in-your-mouth cake.

1 cup butter (no substitutes)
1 8-ounce package cream cheese
6 eggs
3 cups all-purpose flour
1 teaspoon baking powder
¼ teaspoon salt
2¼ cups granulated sugar
¼ cup poppy seed
2 teaspoons vanilla
Lemon Icing

Bring the butter, cream cheese, and eggs to room temperature. Meanwhile, grease and lightly flour a 10-inch tube pan; set aside.

Combine flour, baking powder, and salt. Set aside. In a large mixing bowl beat butter and cream cheese with an electric mixer on medium to high speed about 30 seconds or till softened. Gradually add granulated sugar, 2 tablespoons at a time, beating on medium speed about 5 minutes or till very light and fluffy.

Add poppy seed and vanilla. Add eggs, one at a time, beating on low to medium speed for 1 minute after each addition and scraping bowl frequently. Gradually add flour mixture, beating on low speed just till combined. Pour batter into prepared pan.

Bake in a 325° oven about 1¼ hours or till a wooden toothpick inserted in center comes out clean. Cool in pan on a wire rack for 15 minutes. Remove from pan. Cool completely on wire rack. Drizzle with Lemon Icing. Makes 16 to 20 servings.

Lemon Icing: In a small mixing bowl stir together 1½ cups sifted *powdered sugar,* ½ teaspoon finely shredded *lemon peel,* and enough *lemon juice* (1 to 2 tablespoons) to make an icing of drizzling consistency.

Nutrition information per serving: 415 calories, 6 g protein, 55 g carbohydrate, 19 g fat (11 g saturated), 126 mg cholesterol, 239 mg sodium.

Apple Cake with Caramel-Raisin Sauce

Brighten a cold, gray winter day with a wedge of this moist spice cake generously drizzled with warm caramel sauce.

2   cups all-purpose flour
¾   cup granulated sugar
½   cup packed brown sugar
2   teaspoons baking powder
1   teaspoon ground cinnamon
½   teaspoon baking soda
½   teaspoon salt
½   teaspoon ground ginger
¼   teaspoon ground cloves
2   slightly beaten eggs
1   8-ounce carton dairy sour cream
¼   cup butter or margarine, melted
3   tablespoons milk
1   teaspoon vanilla
1   medium apple, peeled and coarsely
     shredded (1 cup)
⅔   cup chopped walnuts
     Caramel-Raisin Sauce

Grease and lightly flour an 8-inch springform pan or a 9x9x2-inch baking pan; set aside.

In a large mixing bowl stir together the 2 cups flour, granulated sugar, brown sugar, baking powder, cinnamon, baking soda, salt, ginger, and cloves. Make a well in the center of the flour mixture.

In a medium mixing bowl combine eggs, sour cream, melted butter or margarine, milk, and vanilla. Add the egg mixture all at once to flour mixture. Stir just till moistened. Fold in shredded apple and nuts. Spread batter in prepared pan.

Bake in a 350° oven about 50 minutes for springform pan (about 45 minutes for 9-inch pan) or till a wooden toothpick inserted near the center comes out clean. Cool in pan on a wire rack for 20 minutes. Remove side of springform pan. Serve warm or cool with Caramel-Raisin Sauce. Makes 12 servings.

Caramel-Raisin Sauce: In a medium saucepan melt ½ cup *butter or margarine.* Stir in 1 cup packed *brown sugar* and 2 tablespoons *light-colored corn syrup.* Cook and stir over medium heat to a full boil. Stir in ½ cup *whipping cream.* Return to a full boil. Remove from heat. Stir in ¼ cup *raisins.* Serve warm.

Nutrition information per serving: 460 calories, 5 g protein, 58 g carbohydrate, 24 g fat (13 g saturated), 88 mg cholesterol, 355 mg sodium.

Mini Molten Chocolate Cakes

American restaurants made these rich cakes that ooze with chocolate popular; we made them easy.

¾ cup butter
6 ounces semisweet chocolate,
    chopped
    Granulated sugar
3 eggs
3 egg yolks
⅓ cup sifted powdered sugar
1½ teaspoons vanilla
¼ cup all-purpose flour
2 tablespoons unsweetened
    cocoa powder
    Mocha Cream
    Sifted powdered sugar (optional)
    Raspberries (optional)
    Chocolate Spirals (optional)

In a heavy saucepan combine butter and chopped chocolate. Cook and stir over low heat till melted. Remove from heat; cool. Grease six 1-cup soufflé dishes or 6-ounce custard cups. Coat with granulated sugar. Place in a shallow baking pan; set aside.

Beat eggs, egg yolks, ⅓ cup powdered sugar, and vanilla with an electric mixer on high speed about 5 minutes or till thick and pale yellow. Beat in chocolate mixture on medium speed. Sift flour and cocoa powder over chocolate mixture; beat on low speed just till blended. Spoon into prepared dishes.

Bake in a 400° oven for 12 to 14 minutes or till cakes rise slightly and feel firm at edges and softer in centers. Cool in dishes for 5 minutes. Invert onto dessert plates. Cool for 15 minutes. Serve with Mocha Cream. If desired, sprinkle with additional sifted powdered sugar and garnish with raspberries and Chocolate Spirals. Makes 6 servings.

Mocha Cream: Combine 1 teaspoon *instant espresso coffee powder* or 2 teaspoons *instant coffee crystals* and 1 teaspoon *hot water* till dissolved. In a chilled bowl combine ½ cup *whipping cream*, 2 tablespoons sifted *powdered sugar*, 1 teaspoon *unsweetened cocoa powder*, ½ teaspoon *vanilla,* and espresso mixture. Beat with chilled beaters of an electric mixer till soft peaks form.

Chocolate Spirals: Melt 6 ounces *chocolate* and 1 tablespoon *shortening;* cool slightly. Pipe onto waxed paper in spiral shapes. Let dry.

Nutrition information per serving: 532 calories, 8 g protein, 31 g carbohydrate, 45 g fat (26 g saturated), 302 mg cholesterol, 276 mg sodium.

Pumpkin Cake Roll

A spiced cake and crunchy walnuts encircle a cream cheese filling—a perfect fall flavor combination.

3   eggs
1   cup granulated sugar
⅔   cup canned pumpkin
1   teaspoon lemon juice
¾   cup all-purpose flour
2   teaspoons ground cinnamon
1   teaspoon baking powder
1   teaspoon ground ginger
½   teaspoon ground nutmeg
¼   teaspoon salt
1   cup finely chopped walnuts
    Sifted powdered sugar
1   cup sifted powdered sugar
2   3-ounce packages cream cheese,
        softened
¼   cup margarine or butter, softened
½   teaspoon vanilla

Grease and flour a 15x10x1-inch baking pan; set aside. In a large mixing bowl beat eggs with an electric mixer on high speed for 5 minutes. Gradually beat in the granulated sugar. Stir in pumpkin and lemon juice.

In a medium mixing bowl stir together the flour, cinnamon, baking powder, ginger, nutmeg, and salt. Fold into pumpkin mixture. Spread in the prepared pan. Sprinkle with walnuts.

Bake in a 375° oven about 15 minutes or till cake springs back when lightly touched. Immediately loosen edges of cake from pan and turn cake out onto a towel sprinkled with powdered sugar. Starting from a short side, roll up warm cake and towel together. Cool.

For filling, in a medium mixing bowl combine 1 cup powdered sugar, cream cheese, margarine or butter, and vanilla. Beat with an electric mixer on low speed till smooth.

Carefully unroll cooled cake and towel. Spread filling over cake, leaving a 1-inch border around edges. Reroll cake without towel. Cover and chill. To serve, sprinkle with additional powdered sugar. Cut into slices. Makes 10 servings.

Nutrition information per serving: 358 calories, 6 g protein, 42 g carbohydrate, 20 g fat (6 g saturated), 83 mg cholesterol, 209 mg sodium.

Chocolate-Irish Cream Cheesecake

Impress your guests with this home-baked version of a favorite often found on dessert carts in fine restaurants.

1   cup finely crushed chocolate wafers (about 17 cookies)*
¼   cup butter or margarine, melted
½   teaspoon ground cinnamon
3   8-ounce packages cream cheese, softened
1   8-ounce carton dairy sour cream
1   8-ounce package semisweet chocolate, melted and cooled
1   cup sugar
3   eggs
½   cup Irish cream liqueur**
2   tablespoons whipping cream or milk
2   teaspoons vanilla
⅓   cup semisweet chocolate pieces, melted (optional)

For crust, in a small bowl combine crushed wafers, butter or margarine, and cinnamon. Press mixture onto the bottom of an ungreased 9- or 10-inch* springform pan. Set aside.

For filling, in a large bowl beat cream cheese, sour cream, the 8 ounces melted chocolate, and sugar with an electric mixer on medium to high speed till smooth. Add eggs all at once. Beat on low speed just till combined. Stir in liqueur, cream or milk, and vanilla.

Pour into prepared pan. Place in a shallow baking pan. Bake in a 325° oven for 50 to 60 minutes or till center appears nearly set when shaken.

Cool in springform pan on a wire rack for 15 minutes. Loosen the cheesecake from side of pan; cool for 30 minutes more. Remove side of pan; cool for 1 hour. Cover and chill for 4 to 24 hours. To serve, if desired, drizzle cheesecake with the ⅓ cup melted chocolate. Makes 12 to 16 servings.

*Note: If using a 10-inch springform pan, use 1¼ cups crushed chocolate wafers for the crust.

**Note: If you prefer to use less liqueur, substitute whipping cream or milk for some of the liqueur.

Nutrition information per serving: 525 calories, 7 g protein, 34 g carbohydrate, 37 g fat (20 g saturated), 134 mg cholesterol, 295 mg sodium.

Cheesecake Supreme

Check for doneness by gently shaking the pan rather than inserting a knife, which will make a crack. When the cheesecake is done, a 1-inch area in the center still will jiggle a little: this area will firm after cooling. (Also pictured on the cover.)

1¾ cups finely crushed graham crackers
¼ cup finely chopped walnuts
½ teaspoon ground cinnamon
½ cup butter, melted
2 8-ounce packages cream cheese, softened
1 cup sugar
2 tablespoons all-purpose flour
1 teaspoon vanilla
½ teaspoon finely shredded lemon peel (optional)
2 eggs
1 egg yolk
¼ cup milk
 Raspberries (optional)
 Raspberry Sauce (optional)

For crust, combine the graham crackers, walnuts, and cinnamon. Stir in melted butter. If desired, reserve ¼ cup of the crumb mixture for topping. Press the remaining crumb mixture onto the bottom and about 2 inches up the side of an 8- or 9-inch springform pan.

For filling, in a large mixing bowl beat cream cheese, sugar, flour, vanilla, and, if desired, lemon peel with an electric mixer on low speed till combined. Add eggs and egg yolk all at once. Beat on low speed just till combined. Stir in milk. Pour into the prepared pan. If desired, sprinkle with the reserved crumbs.

Place on a shallow baking pan in the oven. Bake in a 375° oven for 45 to 50 minutes for the 8-inch pan (35 to 40 minutes for the 9-inch pan) or till center appears nearly set when shaken.

Cool in pan on a wire rack for 15 minutes. Loosen crust from pan. Cool for 30 minutes more. Remove side of pan. Cool completely. Cover and chill at least 4 hours. If desired, garnish with raspberries and serve with Raspberry Sauce. Makes 12 to 16 servings.

Raspberry Sauce: In a blender container cover and blend 3 cups fresh or thawed, frozen *raspberries* (do not drain), half at a time, till smooth. Press berries through a sieve; discard seeds. In a saucepan combine ⅓ cup *sugar* and 1 teaspoon *cornstarch*. Add sieved berries. Cook and stir till thickened and bubbly. Cook and stir for 2 minutes more. Cool. Makes about 1 cup.

Nutrition information per serving: 429 calories, 7 g protein, 30 g carbohydrate, 32 g fat (18 g saturated), 137 mg cholesterol, 329 mg sodium.

Triple-Chocolate Chunk Cookies

For the true chocoholic, there is no such thing as too much chocolate. These chunky, oversize treats contain a trio of chocolates.

1   cup butter
¾   cup granulated sugar
¾   cup packed brown sugar
1   teaspoon baking soda
2   eggs
1   teaspoon vanilla
3   ounces unsweetened chocolate, melted and cooled
2   cups all-purpose flour
8   ounces semisweet chocolate, cut into ½-inch pieces, or 1⅓ cups large semisweet chocolate pieces
6   ounces white baking bar, cut into ½-inch pieces, or 1 cup white baking pieces
1   cup chopped black walnuts or pecans (optional)

Lightly grease a cookie sheet; set aside. In a large mixing bowl beat butter with an electric mixer on medium to high speed for 30 seconds.

Beat in granulated sugar, brown sugar, and baking soda till combined. Beat in eggs and vanilla till combined. Stir in melted chocolate. Beat in as much of the flour as you can with the mixer. Stir in any remaining flour with a wooden spoon. Stir in the chocolate and white baking pieces and, if desired, nuts.

Using a ¼-cup dry measure or a scoop, drop mounds of dough about 4 inches apart onto the prepared cookie sheet.

Bake in a 350° oven for 12 to 14 minutes or till edges are firm. Cool on cookie sheet for 1 minute. Remove and cool on a wire rack. Makes about 22 cookies.

Nutrition information per cookie: 280 calories, 3 g protein, 33 g carbohydrate, 17 g fat (10 g saturated), 44 mg cholesterol, 158 mg sodium.

Micro-Melting Chocolate

Your microwave oven offers a handy way to melt chocolate. Place up to 6 ounces of chopped chocolate bars, squares, or pieces into a microwave-safe bowl. Micro-cook, uncovered, on 100% power (high) for 1½ to 2 minutes or until soft enough to stir smooth. Stir after every minute during heating. The chocolate will hold its shape after it starts to melt, so stir to see how melted the chocolate is and to help it heat evenly.

Cranberry Pinwheels

Orange marmalade and cranberries team up for a sweet-tart filling in these delightful cookies.

1 cup cranberries
¼ cup orange marmalade
1 tablespoon honey
⅔ cup butter or margarine
½ cup granulated sugar
1 teaspoon baking powder
½ teaspoon finely shredded orange
    peel
1 egg
1 tablespoon milk
1 teaspoon vanilla
2 cups all-purpose flour
    Powdered Sugar Icing
¼ cup finely chopped walnuts

For filling, in a covered small saucepan cook the cranberries, orange marmalade, and honey over low heat till mixture boils and berries pop. Uncover and cook about 8 minutes more or till mixture is the consistency of thick jam, stirring occasionally. Cool.

In a large mixing bowl beat the butter or margarine with an electric mixer on medium to high speed for 30 seconds. Add granulated sugar, baking powder, and orange peel and beat till combined. Beat in egg, milk, and vanilla till combined. Beat in as much of the flour as you can with the mixer. Stir in any remaining flour with a wooden spoon. Divide dough in half. Cover and chill about 3 hours or till easy to handle.

On a lightly floured surface, roll each half of dough into a 10-inch square. Cut each half into sixteen 2½-inch squares. Place squares 2 inches apart on an ungreased cookie sheet. Cut 1-inch slits from each corner to the center of each square. Spoon about ¾ teaspoon of the filling in the center of each square. Fold every other point to the center to form a pinwheel. Pinch points together to seal. (If necessary to seal, lightly moisten points with water.)

Bake in a 375° oven for 8 to 10 minutes or till points just begin to turn brown. Remove and cool on a wire rack. Drizzle with Powdered Sugar Icing. Sprinkle nuts in center of cookies. Makes 32 cookies.

Powdered Sugar Icing: Mix ½ cup sifted *powdered sugar,* 2 teaspoons *milk,* and a few drops *vanilla.* Stir in enough additional *milk,* a small amount at a time, to make an icing of drizzling consistency.

Nutrition information per cookie: 97 calories, 1 g protein, 13 g carbohydrate, 5 g fat (2 g saturated), 17 mg cholesterol, 53 mg sodium.

Citrus-Hazelnut Bars

Definitely a bar cookie with lots of appeal—these double citrus and nutty delights are not overly sweet and make a great accompaniment to an afternoon tea break.

⅓ cup butter
¼ cup granulated sugar
1 cup all-purpose flour
⅓ cup finely chopped hazelnuts
    (filberts) or chopped almonds,
    toasted
2 eggs
¾ cup granulated sugar
2 tablespoons all-purpose flour
1 teaspoon finely shredded orange
    peel
1 teaspoon finely shredded lemon peel
2 tablespoons orange juice
1 tablespoon lemon juice
½ teaspoon baking powder
    Powdered sugar (optional)

For crust, in a medium mixing bowl beat the butter with an electric mixer on medium to high speed for 30 seconds. Add the ¼ cup granulated sugar. Beat till thoroughly combined. Beat in the 1 cup flour and about half of the nuts till mixture is crumbly.

Press mixture onto bottom of an ungreased 8x8x2-inch baking pan. Bake in a 350° oven about 10 minutes or till lightly browned.

Meanwhile, in a medium mixing bowl combine eggs, the ¾ cup granulated sugar, the 2 tablespoons flour, orange and lemon peels, orange juice, lemon juice, and baking powder. Beat on medium speed about 2 minutes or till combined. Pour over hot crust. Sprinkle with the remaining nuts.

Bake about 20 minutes more or till light brown around the edges and center is set. Cool on a wire rack. If desired, sift powdered sugar over top. Cut into bars. Store bars, covered, in the refrigerator. Makes 20 bars.

Nutrition information per bar: 111 calories, 2 g protein, 16 g carbohydrate, 5 g fat (1 g saturated), 25 mg cholesterol, 43 mg sodium.

Cutting Bar Cookies

Bar cookies don't have to be squares or rectangles. Why not triangles or diamonds? For triangles, cut cookies into 2 or 2½-inch squares. Then cut each square in half diagonally. For diamonds, first cut straight lines 1 to 1½ inches apart down the length of the pan. Then cut straight lines 1 to 1½ inches apart diagonally across the pan.

Fruit Tart with Amaretto Creme

Use your 9-inch springform pan for this luscious almond and fruit tart.

Pastry for Single-Crust Pie
Milk
1   tablespoon granulated sugar
1   8-ounce package cream cheese,
      softened
1   3-ounce package cream cheese,
      softened
½   cup amaretto
3   tablespoons brown sugar
½   cup finely chopped almonds, toasted
3   to 4 cups chilled assorted fresh fruit
1   tablespoon granulated sugar

Prepare Pastry for Single-Crust Pie. On a lightly floured surface, roll pastry into an 11-inch circle. Ease into a 9-inch springform pan. Press evenly onto the bottom and 1 inch up side of pan. If desired, flute edge. Generously prick bottom and side with tines of a fork. Line with a double thickness of foil.

Bake in a 450° oven for 5 minutes. Remove foil. Brush edge of pastry with milk. Sprinkle with 1 tablespoon granulated sugar. Bake for 7 to 9 minutes more or till golden. Cool completely in pan on a wire rack.

In a small mixing bowl beat cream cheese, amaretto, and brown sugar with an electric mixer on medium speed till smooth. Stir in almonds. Spread over cooled pastry. Serve immediately or chill up to 4 hours.

To serve, top the cream cheese mixture with desired fruit. Remove side of pan. If desired, remove bottom of pan. Sprinkle the fruit with 1 tablespoon granulated sugar. Makes 8 servings.

Pastry for Single-Crust Pie: In a medium bowl stir together 1¼ cups *all-purpose flour* and ¼ teaspoon *salt.* Using a pastry blender, cut in ⅓ cup *shortening* till pieces are pea-size. Using 4 to 5 tablespoons *cold water,* sprinkle 1 tablespoon water at a time over mixture, gently tossing with a fork till all is moistened. Form dough into a ball.

Nutrition information per serving: 398 calories, 6 g protein, 35 g carbohydrate, 26 g fat (9 g saturated), 51 mg cholesterol, 226 mg sodium.

Nut & Chocolate Chip Tart

Just one bite will convince you to elect this fudgelike, nut-studded tart to your own chocolate hall of fame.

½ of a 15-ounce package (1 crust) folded refrigerated unbaked piecrust
3 slightly beaten eggs
1 cup light-colored corn syrup
½ cup packed brown sugar
⅓ cup butter, melted and cooled
1 teaspoon vanilla
1 cup coarsely chopped salted mixed nuts
½ cup miniature semisweet chocolate pieces
⅓ cup miniature semisweet chocolate pieces
1 tablespoon shortening
Vanilla ice cream (optional)

Let piecrust stand at room temperature according to package directions. Unfold piecrust. Ease into an 11-inch tart pan with a removable bottom. Trim piecrust even with edge of pan. Do not prick piecrust.

For filling, in a large mixing bowl combine eggs and corn syrup. Add the brown sugar, butter, and vanilla, stirring till sugar is dissolved. Stir in nuts and ½ cup chocolate pieces.

Place pan on a baking sheet on oven rack. Carefully pour filling into pan. Bake in a 350° oven about 40 minutes or till a knife inserted near center comes out clean. Cool completely in pan on a wire rack.

To serve, cut tart into wedges and transfer to dessert plates. In a heavy small saucepan cook and stir ⅓ cup chocolate pieces and shortening over low heat till chocolate begins to melt. Immediately remove from heat and stir till smooth. Cool slightly.

Transfer to a small, heavy plastic bag. Snip a very small hole in one corner of the bag. Drizzle the melted chocolate in zigzag lines across each tart wedge. If desired, serve tart with ice cream. Cover and chill any leftover tart up to 2 days. Makes 8 to 10 servings.

Nutrition information per serving: 467 calories, 6 g protein, 56 g carbohydrate, 27 g fat (6 g saturated), 86 mg cholesterol, 192 mg sodium.

Cranberry-Pear Pie

The glazed topping that crowns this fabulous fruit pie is a treat in itself.

1 cup sugar
¼ cup all-purpose flour
1 tablespoon finely shredded
    orange peel
1 teaspoon ground cinnamon
4 medium pears, peeled, cored, and
    sliced (5 cups)
2 cups cranberries
    Pastry for Double-Crust Pie
1 tablespoon butter or margarine,
    cut up
    Glazed Nut Topping
    Sweetened whipped cream
    (optional)

In a large mixing bowl combine sugar, flour, orange peel, and cinnamon. Add pears and cranberries; toss to coat. Set aside.

Prepare Pastry for Double-Crust Pie. On a lightly floured surface, roll out half of the pastry. Ease into a 9-inch pie plate. Fill with the pear mixture. Dot with butter or margarine. Trim bottom pastry to ½ inch beyond edge. Roll out remaining pastry; cut into ½-inch-wide strips. Weave strips on top of filling to make a lattice. Press ends of strips into rim of bottom crust. Fold bottom pastry over strips; seal and flute edge. Cover edge with foil.

Bake in a 375° oven for 25 minutes. Remove foil. Bake for 25 to 30 minutes more or till crust is golden. Spoon Glazed Nut Topping over warm pie. Cool on a wire rack before serving. If desired, serve with whipped cream. Makes 8 servings.

Pastry for Double-Crust Pie: In a large bowl stir together 2 cups *all-purpose flour* and ½ teaspoon *salt*. Using a pastry blender, cut in ⅔ cup *shortening* till pieces are pea-size. Using 6 to 7 tablespoons *cold water*, sprinkle 1 tablespoon water at a time over mixture, gently tossing with a fork till all is moistened. Divide in half. Form each half into a ball.

Glazed Nut Topping: Cook and stir ½ cup chopped *walnuts* in 2 tablespoons *butter* or *margarine* over medium heat till lightly browned. Stir in 3 tablespoons *brown sugar*. Cook and stir till sugar is dissolved. Stir in 1 tablespoon *milk*.

Nutrition information per serving: 529 calories, 5 g protein, 72 g carbohydrate, 27 g fat (7 g saturated), 12 mg cholesterol, 188 mg sodium.

Pumpkin Pecan Pie

Filled with lots of crunchy pecans, this special dessert will become a must at your Thanksgiving celebration.

3   slightly beaten eggs
1   15-ounce can pumpkin
¾   cup sugar
½   cup dark-colored corn syrup
1   teaspoon vanilla
¾   teaspoon ground cinnamon
1   unbaked 9-inch piecrust
1   cup chopped pecans
    Whipped cream (optional)
    Ground cinnamon (optional)

In a medium mixing bowl combine eggs, pumpkin, sugar, corn syrup, vanilla, and ¾ teaspoon cinnamon; mix well. Pour into piecrust. Sprinkle with pecans.

Bake in a 350° oven for 50 to 55 minutes or till a knife inserted near center comes out clean. Cool on a wire rack. Refrigerate within 2 hours; cover for longer storage. If desired, serve pie with whipped cream and sprinkle with additional cinnamon. Makes 8 servings.

Nutrition information per serving: 412 calories, 6 g protein, 55 g carbohydrate, 20 g fat (4 g saturated), 80 mg cholesterol, 108 mg sodium.

Candy Bar Pie

Don't try to cut corners by using a pastry crust—the walnut crust is what makes this pie exquisite. For easier serving, set the frozen pie on a warm, damp towel for a couple of minutes before cutting the first wedge.

6   1- to 1½-ounce bars milk chocolate
     with almonds, chopped
15 large marshmallows or
     1½ cups tiny marshmallows
½   cup milk
1   cup whipping cream
½   teaspoon vanilla
    Walnut Crust
    Whipped cream (optional)
    Coarsely chopped milk chocolate
     bars with almonds (optional)

For filling, in a medium saucepan combine the 6 chopped chocolate bars, marshmallows, and milk. Cook and stir over medium-low heat till chocolate is melted. Remove from heat. Cool to room temperature.

In a chilled large mixing bowl combine the 1 cup whipping cream and vanilla. Beat with chilled beaters of an electric mixer till soft peaks form. Fold into the cooled chocolate mixture. Spoon into Walnut Crust. Freeze about 5 hours or till firm.

To serve, remove from freezer and let stand about 10 minutes before cutting into wedges. If desired, garnish with additional whipped cream and chopped chocolate bars. Makes 8 servings.

Walnut Crust: In a medium bowl combine 1½ cups coarsely ground *walnuts* (6 ounces), 3 tablespoons melted *butter* or *margarine*, and 2 tablespoons *sugar*. Press firmly onto bottom and up the side of a 9-inch pie plate. Bake in a 325° oven about 10 minutes or till edge is golden brown. Cool on a wire rack.

Nutrition information per serving: 440 calories, 6 g protein, 27 g carbohydrate, 36 g fat (12 g saturated), 46 mg cholesterol, 92 mg sodium.

Apple-Blueberry Pastries

Take a platter of these petite pastries to your next potluck.

2 tablespoons sugar

1 tablespoon cornstarch

2 medium apples, peeled, cored, and chopped (about 2 cups)

½ cup fresh or frozen blueberries

1½ teaspoons water

½ teaspoon finely shredded orange peel

1 17¼-ounce package (2 sheets) frozen puff pastry

Easy Orange Icing

Edible flowers (optional)

Line a large baking sheet with foil; set aside. For filling, in a medium saucepan stir together the sugar and cornstarch. Add apples, blueberries, and water. Cook and stir over medium heat till thickened and bubbly. Cook and stir for 2 minutes more. Stir in orange peel. Remove from heat. Cool completely.

Let folded puff pastry thaw at room temperature for 20 minutes. On a lightly floured surface, unfold and roll each sheet of pastry into a 15x10-inch rectangle. Cut each sheet into ten 5x3-inch rectangles.

Spoon about 1 tablespoon of the filling on half of each rectangle to within ½ inch of edges. Brush edges with water. Starting from a short side, lift pastry up and over filling. Press edges with the tines of a fork to seal. Place on the prepared baking sheet.

Bake in a 375° oven for 18 to 20 minutes or till golden. Remove and cool on a wire rack. Drizzle with Easy Orange Icing. If desired, garnish with edible flowers. Makes 20 pastries.

Easy Orange Icing: In a small mixing bowl stir together 1 cup sifted *powdered sugar*, 1 tablespoon *orange juice*, and ¼ teaspoon *vanilla*. Stir in additional *orange juice*, 1 teaspoon at a time, till icing is of drizzling consistency.

Nutrition information per pastry: 142 calories, 1 g protein, 18 g carbohydrate, 8 g fat (0 g saturated), 0 mg cholesterol, 92 mg sodium.

Coffee Éclairs

These sumptuous, tender shells are filled with ice cream and topped with a smooth coffee-flavored sauce.

1   cup water
½   cup butter or margarine
1   cup all-purpose flour
4   eggs
1   quart coffee or vanilla ice cream
1½ cups cold water
3   tablespoons cornstarch
1   tablespoon instant coffee crystals
1   cup light-colored corn syrup
2   tablespoons butter or margarine
1   teaspoon vanilla
½   cup chopped pecans (optional)

Grease a large baking sheet; set aside. In a medium saucepan combine the 1 cup water and ½ cup butter or margarine. Bring to boiling. Add flour all at once, stirring vigorously. Cook and stir till mixture forms a ball that doesn't separate. Remove from heat. Cool for 10 minutes. Add eggs, one at a time, beating well after each addition till smooth.

Spoon dough into a decorating bag fitted with a large plain round tip (about ½-inch opening). Pipe 10 to 12 strips of dough, about 3 inches apart, onto the prepared baking sheet, making each strip about 4 inches long, 1 inch wide, and ¾ inch high.

Bake in a 400° oven about 40 minutes or till golden brown. Remove and cool on a wire rack. Cut éclairs in half lengthwise and remove soft dough from centers. Fill bottom halves with ice cream; replace tops. Cover and freeze till serving time. To serve, remove from freezer and let stand about 15 minutes to soften.

Meanwhile, for sauce, in a medium saucepan combine the 1½ cups cold water, cornstarch, and coffee crystals. Stir in corn syrup. Cook and stir till thickened and bubbly. Cook and stir for 2 minutes more. Remove from heat. Add the 2 tablespoons butter or margarine and vanilla; stir till butter is melted.

Serve some of the warm sauce over éclairs. If desired, sprinkle with pecans. (Cover and chill any leftover sauce up to 1 week. Reheat sauce and serve with ice cream.) Makes 10 to 12 éclairs.

Nutrition information per éclair: 385 calories, 6 g protein, 49 g carbohydrate, 19 g fat (11 g saturated), 139 mg cholesterol, 207 mg sodium.

Frosty Mocha Slices

For a lower-fat version, use reduced-fat cookies, fat-free milk, frozen yogurt, and fat-free pudding mix.

1 cup finely crushed chocolate chip cookies (10 to 12 cookies)
2 tablespoons butter or margarine, melted
½ cup milk
1 to 2 tablespoons instant coffee crystals
1 pint vanilla ice cream
1 4-serving-size package instant vanilla pudding mix

Line a 9x5x3-inch loaf pan with foil. Combine crushed cookies and butter or margarine. Set aside ¼ cup crumbs. Press remaining crumbs into bottom of pan.

Combine milk and coffee crystals, stirring to dissolve. In a medium bowl stir ice cream just to soften. Add milk mixture and pudding mix. Beat with an electric mixer on low speed about 2 minutes or till well mixed and slightly thickened. Pour into crust-lined pan, spreading evenly. Sprinkle with the reserved crumbs. Cover and freeze several hours or till firm.

To serve, remove from freezer and let stand for 10 minutes before slicing. Makes 6 to 8 servings.

Nutrition information per serving: 321 calories, 2 g protein, 44 g carbohydrate, 16 g fat (7 g saturated), 31 mg cholesterol, 302 mg sodium.

Peach-Pecan Ice Cream

Toasting the pecans intensifies their flavor and helps keep them crisp.

3 cups half-and-half or light cream
1½ cups sugar
1 tablespoon vanilla
3 cups whipping cream
4 cups finely chopped peeled peaches or one 16-ounce package frozen unsweetened peach slices, thawed and finely chopped
½ cup chopped pecans, toasted
Peach slices (optional)

In a very large mixing bowl combine half-and-half or light cream, sugar, and vanilla. Stir till sugar is dissolved. Stir in whipping cream. Stir in finely chopped peaches and toasted pecans.

Freeze in a 4- or 5-quart ice-cream freezer according to manufacturer's directions. If desired, garnish with peach slices. Makes 16 servings.

Nutrition information per serving: 329 calories, 3 g protein, 28 g carbohydrate, 24 g fat (14 g saturated), 78 mg cholesterol, 35 mg sodium.

Frosty Chocolate-Cherry Yogurt

Yogurt swirled with cherries and chocolate makes a cool, creamy, and scrumptious alternative to ice cream.

2   16-ounce cartons (3½ cups) vanilla
    yogurt (no gelatin added)*
2½ cups fresh or frozen pitted dark
    sweet cherries
⅓   cup milk
⅓   cup light-colored corn syrup
½   cup miniature semisweet
    chocolate pieces
    Fresh dark sweet cherries (optional)

In a blender container or food processor bowl combine yogurt, 1 cup of the pitted cherries, milk, and corn syrup. Cover and blend or process till almost smooth. (If using a food processor, process half at a time.)

Freeze in a 2-quart ice-cream freezer according to manufacturer's directions till almost firm. Add the remaining pitted cherries and chocolate. Continue to freeze as directed till firm. If desired, serve with additional fresh cherries. Makes 12 servings.

*Note: Yogurt without gelatin gives this dessert a better texture. Check the ingredients on the label.

Nutrition information per serving: 299 calories, 8 g protein, 55 g carbohydrate, 8 g fat (2 g saturated), 9 mg cholesterol, 107 mg sodium.

English Toffee Ice Cream

If you're making this frozen treat for kids, substitute milk for the coffee.

4   1.4-ounce bars chocolate-covered
    English toffee
2   cups whipping cream
1   14-ounce can sweetened
    condensed milk
½   cup strong coffee, cooled
1½ teaspoons vanilla

Crush toffee bars by placing them between two pieces of waxed paper and crushing them with a rolling pin. Set aside. Combine the whipping cream, sweetened condensed milk, coffee, and vanilla. Chill.

Beat with an electric mixer on low speed till slightly thickened. Fold in toffee. Spoon into a 2-quart square baking dish or a 9x5x3-inch loaf pan. Cover and freeze several hours or till firm. Makes 12 servings.

Nutrition information per serving: 315 calories, 4 g protein, 27 g carbohydrate, 21 g fat (12 g saturated), 68 mg cholesterol, 94 mg sodium.

Frosty Chocolate-Cherry Yogurt

Ginger Custard with Plum Sauce

For a rosy red sauce, choose a variety of plums with red skin, such as Red Beaut, Ace, or Queen Ann.

4   slightly beaten eggs
2   cups milk
½   cup sugar
1   teaspoon vanilla
½   teaspoon ground ginger
6   fresh medium plums, pitted and
       coarsely chopped (2½ cups)
⅓   cup sugar
1   tablespoon lemon juice
1   tablespoon water
1½ teaspoons cornstarch
½   teaspoon vanilla

In a medium mixing bowl combine eggs, milk, ½ cup sugar, 1 teaspoon vanilla, and ginger. Beat till well combined but not foamy. Place six 6-ounce custard cups in a large shallow baking pan on oven rack. Pour egg mixture into custard cups. Pour hot water into pan around custard cups to reach halfway up sides of cups.

Bake in a 350° oven for 30 to 35 minutes or till a knife inserted near centers comes out clean. Remove cups from water. Cool on a wire rack at least 20 minutes.

Meanwhile, for plum sauce, in a medium saucepan combine plums, ⅓ cup sugar, and lemon juice. Bring to boiling; reduce heat. Cover and simmer about 8 minutes or till plums are tender. Stir together water and cornstarch. Stir into plum mixture. Cook and stir till thickened and bubbly. Cook and stir for 2 minutes more. Remove from heat. Stir in ½ teaspoon vanilla.

To serve, unmold custards onto dessert plates. Spoon plum sauce over custards. Makes 6 servings.

Nutrition information per serving: 241 calories, 7 g protein, 42 g carbohydrate, 5 g fat (2 g saturated), 148 mg cholesterol, 83 mg sodium.

Perfectly Ripe Plums

To purchase plums at their peak, look for firm, plump, well-shaped fruit with good color for its variety. Press a plum gently; it should give slightly. The bloom (light gray cast) on the skin is natural protection and doesn't affect quality. Avoid overly soft, bruised, or very hard fruit. To ripen plums at home, store at room temperature for 1 to 2 days. Then refrigerate them for up to 5 days.

Orange Bread Pudding with Warm Maple Sauce

So much flavor, so little fat—this bread pudding seemingly has it all.

4 slices white or whole wheat bread
⅓ cup raisins
3 eggs
2 egg whites
1¾ cups milk
⅓ cup orange marmalade
¼ cup sugar
½ teaspoon ground cinnamon
½ teaspoon vanilla
Maple Sauce
Orange slices, halved

Cut bread into 2-inch strips. Spread strips in a large shallow baking pan. Bake in a 325° oven for 10 to 15 minutes or till dry, stirring twice. Transfer strips to an ungreased 8x1½-inch round baking pan. Sprinkle with raisins. Set aside.

In a medium mixing bowl beat together eggs, egg whites, milk, orange marmalade, sugar, cinnamon, and vanilla with a wire whisk, fork, or rotary beater. Pour over bread and raisins in pan.

Bake in the 325° oven about 55 minutes or till a knife inserted near the center comes out clean. Cool slightly on a wire rack. Serve warm with warm Maple Sauce and garnish with orange slices. Makes 6 servings.

Maple Sauce: In a saucepan combine 1 tablespoon *cornstarch* and ¼ teaspoon finely shredded *orange peel*. Stir in ¾ cup *orange juice* and ⅓ cup *maple-flavored syrup*. Cook and stir till thickened and bubbly. Cook and stir for 2 minutes more. Remove from heat. Stir in 1 teaspoon *butter* or *margarine*. Makes about 1 cup.

Nutrition information per serving: 299 calories, 9 g protein, 56 g carbohydrate, 5 g fat (2 g saturated), 113 mg cholesterol, 187 mg sodium.

Rice Pudding

This creamy rice pudding is a soothing conclusion to a spicy meal.

½ cup golden raisins
¼ cup rum
3 cups milk
½ cup long grain rice
3 inches stick cinnamon
¼ cup sugar
1 teaspoon vanilla
  Ground cinnamon

In a small bowl combine raisins and rum. Set aside. In a heavy medium saucepan combine milk, uncooked rice, and stick cinnamon. Bring to boiling; reduce heat. Cover and simmer about 20 minutes or till rice is tender. Remove stick cinnamon.

Drain raisins, discarding rum. Stir the raisins, sugar, and vanilla into rice mixture. Sprinkle with ground cinnamon. Serve warm or chilled. Makes 6 servings.

Nutrition information per serving: 200 calories, 6 g protein, 38 g carbohydrate, 3 g fat (2 g saturated), 9 mg cholesterol, 64 mg sodium.

Brownie Pudding

As this homey dessert bakes, a layer of cake magically rises to the top, leaving a chocolaty sauce underneath.

1 cup all-purpose flour
¾ cup granulated sugar
2 tablespoons unsweetened cocoa
    powder
2 teaspoons baking powder
¼ teaspoon salt
½ cup milk
2 tablespoons cooking oil
1 teaspoon vanilla
½ cup chopped walnuts
¾ cup packed brown sugar
¼ cup unsweetened cocoa powder
1½ cups boiling water

Grease an 8x8x2-inch baking pan; set aside. In a medium mixing bowl stir together flour, granulated sugar, 2 tablespoons cocoa powder, baking powder, and salt. Stir in milk, oil, and vanilla. Stir in walnuts.

Pour into the prepared pan. In another medium bowl stir together brown sugar and ¼ cup cocoa powder. Stir in the boiling water; slowly pour over batter. Bake in a 350° oven for 40 minutes. Cool on a wire rack for 45 to 60 minutes. Serve warm. Makes 6 to 8 servings.

Nutrition information per serving: 368 calories, 5 g protein, 65 g carbohydrate, 12 g fat (2 g saturated), 2 mg cholesterol, 271 mg sodium.

Cinnamon Meringues with Fruit

For crispy meringue shells, serve them right away. However, if you like softer, marshmallow-like shells, chill them for up to 2 hours before serving.

2 egg whites
½ teaspoon ground cinnamon
½ teaspoon vanilla
¼ teaspoon cream of tartar
½ cup sugar
2 cups sliced peeled peaches or sliced nectarines
2 tablespoons sugar
1 tablespoon cornstarch
2 cups fresh fruit (such as sliced peeled peaches or kiwifruit and/or sliced nectarines or strawberries)

For meringue shells, cover a baking sheet with plain brown paper (specially made for baking). Draw six 3-inch squares or six 3½-inch circles on the paper. In a small mixing bowl beat the egg whites, cinnamon, vanilla, and cream of tartar with an electric mixer on medium speed till soft peaks form. Gradually add the ½ cup sugar, beating on high speed till stiff peaks form and sugar is almost dissolved.

Spoon meringue mixture into a decorating bag fitted with a medium plain-round or star tip (about ¼-inch opening). Pipe shells onto the prepared baking sheet. (Or, using a spoon or a spatula, spread the meringue mixture over the squares or circles on the prepared baking sheet, building up sides to form shells.)

Bake in a 300° oven for 30 minutes. Turn off the heat and let shells dry in the oven with the door closed for at least 1 hour. (Do not open oven.) Peel off paper.

For sauce, place 2 cups peaches or nectarines in a blender container or food processor bowl. Cover and blend or process till nearly smooth. Pour into a saucepan. Mix 2 tablespoons sugar and cornstarch; stir into peach mixture. Cook and stir till thickened and bubbly. Cook and stir for 2 minutes more.

To serve, place meringue shells on dessert plates. Spoon the sauce into meringue shells. Top with fresh fruit. Serve immediately or cover and chill up to 2 hours. Makes 6 servings.

Nutrition information per serving: 138 calories, 2 g protein, 34 g carbohydrate, 0 g fat (0 g saturated), 0 mg cholesterol, 19 mg sodium.

INDEX